The Limerickiad

The Limerickiad
volume one: from Gilgamesh to Shakespeare
Martin Rowson

Published 2011 by
Smokestack Books
PO Box 408, Middlesbrough TS5 6WA
e-mail: info@smokestack-books.co.uk
www.smokestack-books.co.uk

The Limerickiad
volume one: from Gilgamesh to Shakespeare
Copyright 2011 by Martin Rowson
Cover illustration: Martin Rowson

Printed by
EPW Print & Design Ltd

ISBN 978-0-9568144-2-5
Smokestack Books gratefully
acknowledges the support of
Arts Council England

Smokestack Books is
represented by Inpress Ltd
www.inpressbooks.co.uk

Thanks are due to the *Independent on Sunday*, where most of these poems first appeared.

Contents

Dedication

The word 'Poet' still tends to lodge a
View of some romantic codger,
      A craftsman who'll render
      Lines witty, wise, tender,
While a LIMERICK's penned by a BODGER.

So, as Limerick Bodger, I'm blessed
By two editors, up with the best
      On THE SINDY! Hooray
      For divine SUZI FEAY
And her successor dear KATY GUEST!

Though she scorns my poor poems, God knows,
This DEDICATION, I propose
      To extend in like manner
      To my darling wife ANNA,
Plus our children – to wit, FRED and ROSE!

Gilgamesh

How can we make Lit. Hist. seem fresh?
By WRITING IN LIMERICKS to mesh
        The genres and fit
        In the WHOLE OF WORLD LIT
Starting off with GILGAMESH.

This first written tale, all concur,
Was scratched on clay tablets in Ur
        Though I won't be comparian
        The Akkadian and Sumerian.
That's above my paygrade, I aver.

We can guess his was hardly a puny form*
And he probably wore a nice uniform
        Though I doubt we can figure that
        He lived in a ziggurat.
That's the problem with translating cuneiform.

*Whether man or god, here I'm assumin'
We agree here that to Ur is human…

Papyri

Up next in our quest of inquiry
We grapple with Egypt's PAPYRI
       Filled with hieroglyphic.
       To be more specific,
Do we know this stuff wasn't a *DIARY?*

Though Political diaries are chronic
They might not be if they're PHARONIC!
       Penned by TUTENKHAMUN
       Such screeds might prove charmin'
(If you don't read the 'glyph as a *phonic*).

For would not, say, CAMPBELL be better*
With an eye or a bird for each letter?
       Like THE BOOK OF THE DEAD
       He could not be read
Without cribs from the Stone of Rosetta!

* (This applies to the whole sodding cannon
From ALAN CLARK back to CHIPS CHANNON!
And with my conceit, if you please,
This oeuvre now includes RAMESES!)

The Old Testament

If Ancient Lit is to prove viable
Through the centuries it must be liable
      To thrill *and* to sell,
      And to spook you to hell.
And thus we arrive at *The Biable*.*

Creation, the Law, some Astronomy,
From Genesis to Deuteronomy:
      Basically, Yahweh
      Said, 'We did it our way!'
Though it hardly o'erbrims with true bonhomie.

This bestseller's best points? It conquers
Hearts and minds from Judea to Yonkers,
      Plus plaguing C. HITCHENS
      With violent twitchins
And driving R. DAWKINS quite bonkers.**

*If this spelling looks weird, please relax.
It's kosher, so says the *Tanakh*.

**Here I bat away every rebuke
That I'm glossing o'er The Pentateuch.
These are LIMERICKS, twelve to the dollar,
And *cheap*. So, no BIBLICAL SCHOLAR.

Homer

Young PARIS cried plaintively, '*Rilly*, dad!
I *love* her!' KING PRIAM thought, 'Silly lad!
      This tosh – girl meets boy –
      Will mean trouble for Troy!'
As you'll find out if you read THE ILIAD.

Proving, when you court Greek King's fillies
You'll get AGAMEMNON, ACHILLES,
      HECTOR *and* The Gods,
      So don't count the odds
Against CASS-ANDRA getting the willies.

Blind HOMER sang of things you godda see
Like sieges, sulks, heels and slain bodies – eeee!
      Not forgetting, of course,
      That absurd Trojan Horse!
Can't wait for his sequel – THE ODYSSEY!

Greek Tragedy

Greek Tragedy proves life is dire.
It says so in THE ORESTEIA.
        Fate evens the score as
        Some bloke from the Chorus
Moans on as he plucks at a lyre.

These dramas all managed to pack in a
Night at the theatre lackin' a
        Laugh or a smile,
        And then after a while
Along comes a DEUS EX MACHINA.

Each trag. (unlike what bedroom farce is)
Tells a story of woe that surpasses
        The Lives of the KENNEDYS!
        Oh, here's the Eumenides.
If you're lucky you might reach Catharsis.

The Greeks

In this tour of Lit's mountainous peaks
We haven't yet got past the Greeks!
      If we stick at this rate – oh!
      We won't get past PLATO
And twelve philosophical cliques.

Nor can we delay to be graphic
About the Pindaric or Sapphic
      Nor take a quick gander
      At chaps like MENANDER.
Life's too short to be so specafic.

So forget all about ARISTOTLE!
HERODOTUS too! I mean, what'll
      It do if cacophanies
      By old ARISTOPHANES
Stop us heading for ROME at full throttle?

The Romans

Though the Romans died years ago, see 'em
Guide our Lit from the morning till pm.
> Judges judging old lags
> Still employ Latin tags
So we might as well too. *Carpe diem!*

Quipped by wits, sung by *bassi profundi*,
It works from Iraq to Burundi,
> So when facing disastra,
> *Per ardua ad astra!**
Sic transit Gloria Mundi!

Dictum sapienti sat est!
Thanks to HORACE and VIRGIL we're blessed,
> And know what the score is:
> *O tempora! O mores!*
For God's sake just give it a rest...

*alternative translation:
Or when stuck in a crevice
Ars longa vita brevis

21

Latin

You know you can't parse, say, Stonehenge,
Yet the Ancient World's wrought its revenge.
        Generations have sat in
        Cold rooms reading Latin
From Alexandria to Penge.

Declining CAESAR's GALLIC WARS
Means not 'No, thank you!' but ensures
        Despair and disgrace!
        Blame the ablative case
And the nominative vocative clause.

The Etruscans just left the odd shard
And all Carthage's Lit was too charred,
        So why did the Roman
        (Though the Tiber was foamin')
Leave us Lit that is so bloody hard?

The Aeneid

Latin verse's great work, THE AENEID,
Tells how from Troy AENEAS had flee-ed
       And took Great Queen DIDO
       Along for the ride. Oh,
It's just Romanised Homer! Agree-ed?

And we all know that VIRGIL was crawling
To the Emperor. That's just appalling.
       Bugger CAESAR AUGUSTUS!
       As for Rome, you must trust us:
Let's skip to Declining and Falling!

But first METAMORPHOSES by OVID.
In insurance terms you should be covid
       If you say to the god
       Who's transforming your bod:
'Just look at this face. Am I bovid?'

St Augustine

Latin Lit spawned both poets and sages
Whose mss filled MMs of pages,
   Or rather great scrolls
   You could read through the hols.
But then along came the Dark Ages.

Why? Well, they'd been pagan and bodily,
But now became Christians. Oddily,
   Once nosh for a lion,
   They trumpeted Zion
And everyone came on all godily!

Boethius felt he'd been blessed
And then St AUGUSTINE confessed
   'Though it's been a great trip
   Now I'm Hippo, not hip!'
No wonder Rome fell (in the West).

The Barbarians

Have you ever occasionally wondered
While barbarian hordes raped and plundered
      With such devilish speed
      What was there to read
Between Rome's Fall and round, say, 800?

The Oral traditions of Goth
Grant no books from that era of Wrath
      So we can't get a handle
      On novels in Vandal
(Which recited sound more like a cough.)

Indeed, Ostrogoth Lit was quite minimal
While the Jutish output was subliminal
      And though verse by the Hun
      Has its moments of fun
Their scansion was frankly quite criminal!

Beowulf

When a Saxon Bard boellowed out 'HWAET!'
It meant 'Harken!' or maybe 'Be qwaet!'
        And the atmosphere sours:
        This means BEOWULF for hours!
I'm surprised that there wasn't a raet!*

Cried the Aelthings, 'We've haerd it beofoer!
Grendel's mum in beocomyng a boer!
        We cannot endure a
        Sec moer of caesura
Or yoer metrycal tricks! Please no moer!'

The Bard, fearful his croewd mycght disperse
Yelled 'Okay! Here's a different verse!
        As yeou're really so crude
        Haere's THE DREAM OF THE ROOD!'
But if aenythyng that one was worse.

*Old English is frankly a mess
Depending on accent and stress
        Plus more letters as well!
        Jaesus Khryste! Bloewddy Hel!
What it means now is anyone's guess.

27

Historia Ecclesiastica Gentis Anglorum

In a monastery south of the Tweed,
'Neath a roof made of wattle and reed
       Where you froze to the marrow
       (Our location is Jarrow)
Sat a monk named the Venerable BEDE.

As his fingertips started to bleed
He considered his lengthening screed
       And thought 'This is fantastical,
       Writing Ecclesiastical
Histories *when no one can read!*'

And the ANGLO-SAXON CHRONICLE agreed*
In the kind of review you don't need:
       'St CUTHBERT is better
       At the illumined letter.'
'Oh sod it!' cried BEDE. 'Pass the mead!'

*And as to the matter of scansion,
If you live in a palace or mansion
       It's all very well,
       But when stuck in a cell
There's always some room for expansion...

The Vikings

The poetical side of the Norse
Is seldom apparent, of course,
   As they ransacked great abbeys
   And filleted babbies
And murdered and raped sans remorse.

It is shown, nonetheless, in the Saga*,
About SNORRI and HARALD HARDRAGA
   Despite their capacity
   For ceaseless rapacity
And burning books quaffing down lager.

So when spying longboats in the dunes
Remember this Lit, writ in runes
   And this Viking Proclivity
   To show sensitivity
Though it's wisest to still hide the spoons.

*The Saga I talk about here
Are those epics of bloodshed and fear
   And wars and disease
   And not OAPs
On a coach trip. I hope that's now clear.

Norse Saga

Here's a Saga, translated from Norse:
Snugrund, son of Cnut, son of Frose,
> *Roared revenge through the fjord*
> *Against Eric Bloodsword**
And then beat out the brains of his horse.

Then did Eric slay Snugrund, whose daughter
Fair Fnari was slain when they brought her
> *To slay Eric's son Sweyne*
> *Who slew Snugrund (again)*
And set off five decades of slaughter.

Till Snog, son of Snogson, Sweyne's son,
Said to Sven, Snugrund's grandson, 'It's fun,
> *I know, to* make feud,
> *But let's cool it, hey dude?'*
Replied Sven, 'But we've hardly begun!'

*Eric, Knork's son, son of Smo,
Son of Hragason, known as Bloodhoe,
> Son of Hragg, son of Hnak,
> Son of Pnagg, son of Svak,
Son of Hrvnak, had once trod on Cnut's toe.

Arthurian

From the High to the Late Middle Ages
You'll observe how each author engages
    With ARTHUR's Round Table
    To read (if you're able)
Across hundreds of thousands of pages.

There's the tale of TRISTAN and ISOLDA
Who gave poor King MARK the cold shoulder.
    Both croaked! Lord above!
    But then that's Courtly Love
As any poor swain could have told 'er.

But there's much more! MERLIN and PENDRAGON,
The Sangreal (a flash kind of flagon),
    PARSIFAL, Swords in Stone,
    LAUNCELOT (and I own
You're a saint if you stay on the wagon)

Not forgetting GAWAIN and Green Knights,
GUINEVERE, MORDRED and fights!
    ARTHUR cried, 'I once thought
    This was fun. Now I'm MORT!
Will the last one to leave kill the lights?'

The Normans

In that year of woe 1066
English Lit found itself in a fix.
>The conquering Norman
>Cried 'Verse is a bore, man!'
And so looked elsewhere for his kicks.

With the market depressed, the King yells
'Who on Earth wants to read Books of Kells?
>Poets! Get in your noodle
>That now that we're feudal
We need something commercial that sells!'

So they sold out, though selling out reeks,
And THE DOMESDAY BOOK's narrative creaks.
>But alas, truth be told
>The damned thing outsold
WILLIAM of MALMSBURY in weeks!

(While the Normans burnt village and hovel
And made all the peasantry grovel
>In distant Bayeux
>They compounded our woe
By inventing the first graphic novel.)

33

Historia Regum

A fellow from Monmouth called Geoff
Wrote of Great British Kings' life and death,
      And of ARTHUR and MERLIN
      (He weren't no H. SPURLIN')
Till his antepenultimate breath.

But Henry of Huntingdon town
Read Geoff with a deepening frown.
      'You call this a chronicle?
      It's more like McGONAGALL!
This so-called historian's a clown!

As for Adam of Usk and those boys
Like Gerald of Wales, their stuff cloys!
      Because, to be exact,
      They claim legends as fact,
And the same goes for CHRETIEN DE TROYES!'*

*Back then, of course, rhyme was a foggy 'un,
Trying chronicler and theologian,
      Since HISTORIA REGUM
      Was a true rhyme for 'phlegm
And don't even *think* MABINOGION.

Langue d'Oc

When knights old and bold fought with lance
There began to appear in South France
      Packs of Troubadours
      Those capering bores
Who'd pluck at their lutes, sing and prance.

They sang in Romance, and this language can
Accommodate a metrical scheme that allows this line to scan.
      They sang songs of chivalry,
      Engaged in fierce rivalry
(And you'll find that those lines rhyme in Occitan).

These Troubadours could be quite funny
But died out although, like BUGS BUNNY
      They would sneer, scoff and mock –
      Though 'What's Up, Langue d'Oc?'
Was beyond their prowess, for my money.

And being quite honest I wouldn't care
If a chain-mailed foot booted the derriere
      Of each simpering ponce
      From Poitou to Provence
And the same thing goes for their Chansonnier!

The Mystery Plays

In that world where a poor peasant farmer
Tilled strips while a pilgrim or palmer
      Heard cathedral bells chime
      It's about bloody time
That we got round to dealing with Drama.

But while the poor serfs were a-sewing
No one planned for THE CLOUD OF UNKNOWING
      To transfer up West.
      As to plays – yes, you've guessed.
There were practically none of them showing.

Save in York, Wakefield, Lincoln and Chester
Where they'd all perform, once a semester
      On the Feast of St Michael
      A MYSTERY CYCLE
To provide some relief from the jester.

A Guild of the Townsfolk would run it
And although this might ruin the fun it
      Was hardly a Mystery
      In this Biblical History
To reveal it was JUDAS whodunnit.

The Divine Comedy

There once was a fellow called DANTE
Who drank too much Asti Spumante
        (Or it may have been Pernod)
        And went to INFERNO
Though most folk prefer Alicante.

He cried 'I don't want to be preachy
But I've lost my girl! She was so peachy,
        Though just over 11.
        I'll scour Hell and Heaven
Until I find my BEATRICE!'

So, aged 35, dodging foamin'
Beasts as he trolled through the gloamin'
        (And if this sounds like Panto
        It's just the first Canto)
He bumped into VIRGIL the Roman.

Who said, 'I will help you, you geek!
Here's the Gate of Hell! Gawd, this is bleak!
        See that sign? GIVE UP HOPE... –
        Watch out, mate! That's a Pope! –
...ALL YE ENTERING HERE! What a cheek!

'You see, in Purgatoria a purge will
Sort it, but we shan't emerge till
        We've seen torment as well
        In the Circles of Hell!
To the FIRST CIRCLE sharpish!' said VIRGIL.

'Now we're though Hell's Gate, rightly despairin',
Observe yonder glum ferryman, starin'.
      You see, if you've died,
      Then to reach the far side
You need *him*. Let me introduce CHARON!'

Quoth the ferryman, 'Gents, I don't give a
Lift as a rule to a liver.
      Besides, the names CHARON!'
      'Alright! Keep your hair on!
Just take us both South of the River!'

Thus VIRGIL and DANTE reached Limbo
Where the unbaptised lolled, arms akimbo.
      'This is too tame,' sighed DANTE.
      Yelled VIRGIL, 'Avanti!
Let's get to the lech and the bimbo!'

Dans le deuxieme circle d'Inferno
The Lustful are *tossed* as the winds blow
      (Ce n'est pas soixante-neuf)
      For their sins back on Earth.
Just hear PAOLO and FRANCESCA howl so!

Fran cried: 'I'm the saddest of women. We
Were lovers, it's true, back in Rimini.
      Though this torment be worthy,
      There weren't nothing pervy!
He never suggested, like, rimmin' me!'

Having heard quite enough Dant departed
For the Third Circle where the downhearted
        Gluttons, now dud,
        Were packed tight in cold mud.
Dante fled before one of them farted.

Then down in the Fourth Circle misers
Pushed round weights of various sizes
        (Though the text is ambiguous
        A circle, contiguous
Contained their Financial Advisers...)

Now DANTE looked down on The Styx,
The Fifth Circle of Hell where they mix
        The Wrathful and Lazy
        (I know this sounds crazy,
But that's how the damned get their kicks).

On the surface the angry brought grief
To each other while just underneath
        The Slothful and Sullen
        Lay gurglin' 'n' mullin'
On the pratfalls of Christian belief.

From the Styx to the Stygian Marsh
Dant and VIRGIL then warily parsh
        (And no wonder they lisp
        As the damned get more crisp
And conditions grow even more harsh!)

Past the Furies they speedily dart
To the City of Dis, spelt in Art
        With one 's', unlike Diss
        In Fair Norfolk, though this
Is the one way to tell them apart.

Through the Sixth Circle, in Dis's walls,
Our man Dante now edgily crawls,
        Past laymen and clerisy
        Who, guilty of heresy,
Lie in Flaming Tombs, singeing their smalls.

And in Hell Circle Numero Seven
It's nastier than 9/11!
        With the Violent immersed
        In boiling blood, cursed
By the merciful judgement of Heaven!

If you think that *that's* gaudy, then next
Come the Suicides, ceaselessly vexed
        And transformed into TREES,
        Torn by Harpies – *Pur-leeze!*
All the readers are now nervous wrecks!

But before one impatiently flings
This book on the fire there are things
        You can do. Think of ELFS
        And not BLACK or WHITE GUELPHS
And it's just like the Lord of the Rings!

In Hell's Seventh Circle the Inner Ring
Allows Dante to hear a poor sinner sing:
        'Oh lawks! Oh alas for me!
        I've been nicked for Blasphemy!'
And nor will the Sodomites win a thing

Save the knowledge that they, praise the Lord,
Like the Usurers, ain't earned reward
        Of the kind that you'll find
        In the Eight Circle. Mind,
That's got *Ten Ditches* in it! Oh Gawd!

They deal with the Frauds in these Bolgia,
Be it Pope, Politician or Soldier:
        Boiled in pitch, drowned in *merde*,
        All these newly interred
Had it coming, as I could've toldya.

Here are Hypocrites, Alchemists, Thieves,
And over there Dante perceives...
        Could it be? No! Shhh! Schtum it!
        THE PROPHET MOHAMET!!
Our hero now sensibly leaves...

At last Dant gains Hell Circle Nine,
The deepest pit wherein repine
        The Traitors (not nice)
        To their necks froze in Ice!
Far too good for these treacherous swine!

But betray your boss, then this foul crime
Sends you to the LAST CIRCLE, you slime!
       Like BRUTUS or JUDAS
       Who end up as food as
They're chewed by Old Nick for all time!

Then it's Purgat'ry, then he's escorted
By BEATRICE through PARADISE! Sorted!!
       Though without any gore
       They're a bit of a bore,
These cantos, or so it's reported.

So does DANTE's shtik come up to par
In *COMEDIC* terms? It ain't ha-ha
       Or laugh-out-loud funny
       Although for my money
It knocks spots off, say, JIMMY CARR...

The Decameron

All of old Dante's harsh hammerin'
Of the SOUL OF MAN's left us all clammerin'
> To get out of this rut
> With some old fashioned smut!
So let's hasten to THE DECAMERON.

These filthy tales, penned by BOCCACCIO
Are purportedly told by a batch, we know,
> Of folk, out of breath
> Who had fled the Black Death
To avoid going 'Ah-ah-ah-TACCIO!'

The stories are told through the prism
Of FORTUNE and LOVE (plus some jism)
> But though steamy and hot
> Bocc had nicked every plot,
So it's less PLAGUE and more PLAGIARISM.

But who are we now to spread blame?
Nicking plots was the name of the game!
> Stolen ideas, perforce, are –
> From SHAKESPEARE to CHAUCER –
Quite standard. D. CAMERON's the same...

Aquinas

While we're still here in the QUATTROCENTO*
I should deal with some stuff that I meantto
      Cover sooner. Apologies.
      Although these theologies
I know bugger all of (I'll pretendto).

For there's no theologian as fine as
That scholar and saint T. AQUINAS
      Who cried 'What a bummer!
      My Theologica (Summa)
Has been marked down as 'A' triple minus!

'I blame that DUNS SCOTUS, who once
Disputed my dicta! Well, cunts
      Like that prove what swine'll
      Accept as doctrinal!
No wonder they called the man DUNCE!

'But ABELARD now! He did blaze a
Trail that would frankly amaze a
      Chap, though 'tis stated
      Poor Pete got castrated!
Possibly by Occam's Razor...'

*I recognise I may have blundered
And mistranslated '1300'...

The Mystics

While we're still in the High Middle Ages
We mustn't forget Mystics. Pages
       Of Mystical Teaching
       Prove GOD is worth reaching
So long as your soul, like, engages.

Though in truth each Monk or Anchoress
Was frankly a bit of a mess,
       with *hairshirts* and *fasting*
       So that Life Everlasting
Must have been a relief, I should guess.

For JULIAN OF NORWICH's cell
Was infused with a musty, damp smell.
       Still, '*All shall be well,*
       And all shall be well,
And all manner of things shall be well!'

But who was she kidding? A tip:
Just take drugs for a similar trip.
       'I know where the hemp is!'
       Cried THOMAS á KEMPIS,
Then crept to the crypt for a kip.

Petrarch

There once was this bloke called PETRARCH
Who leered 'I just fancy a lark!
        And as I adore a
        Hot chick name of LAURA,
Let's go for a romp in the park!

'But first there's my chores, doncha know,
Rehabilitating CICERO!
        I must counter complacence!
        Invent the Renaissance
Through the works of those blokes long ago!

'Then there's Humanism to create
Before I go out, and it's late!
        Though I reach for my bonnet,
        I *must* write a sonnet!
I'll *never* get laid at this rate!'

For see how the heavens now darken
As the nightingales chorus – o harken!
        And anyway LAURA
        Is merely an *aura!*
Heavy petting just isn't *Petrarchan...*

Cleanness and *Pearl*

Medieval Artwork that we treasure
Sometimes leaves out stuff lacking in pleasure.
       Why TRISTAN and YSEULT
       When the Peasants' Revolt
And the Black Death are there for good measure?

You see, while the Literature's rich,
Life was nasty and short, and a bitch.
       Unsurprising, therefore,
       That religion was sure
To make poets churn out loads of kitsch.

I don't want to appear as a churl
But honestly, CLEANNESS or PEARL
       Are precious and mawkish!
       I'm not being hawkish
In saying this stuff makes me hurl!

Life was coarse, so the LIT should be coarser:
Sing of filth in a voice getting hoarser!
       Bin each Book of the Hour,
       Along with JOHN GOWER
And let's get stuck into some CHAUCER!

The Canterbury Tales

'Whan that April with his soures soote...'
What?! Let's try that in English – it's cuter.
      'When it's raining in Spring...'
      Right! Well, then it's the thing
To drink wine out of jugs made of pewter!

But back when Olde Englande was Merrie
It seems that the thing do to very
      Often instead
      Was to leap out of bed
For a PILGRIMAGE to CANTERBURY!

Thus the pilgrims (whanne sonne he dydde shynne)
Went to Kent for to visit the shrine
      Of St THOMAS á BECKET
      And on the way – feck it! –
Told tales (I'd have stuck to the wine).

So that's how THE CANTERBURY TALES
Came about, although here my wit fails:
      Why did they (give me strength)
      Have to talk at such *length?*
Thank God they weren't going to Wales!

So there was this KNIGHT, old and gentle,
And a MILLER and REEVE – this sounds mental –
      Plus a COOK, MAN OF LAW,
      WIFE OF BATH who all tour
By horse as they had no car rental.

In Kent, with a SUMMONER and FRIAR,
They went, although I'd be a liar
      To say that that's *all:*
      There's a CLERK, what they call
A FRANKLIN, PHYSICIAN and SQUIRE,

YOU REALISE WE'RE NOT EVEN AT THE END of THE OLD KENT ROAD YET....

A PARDONER and then – go on! Guess!
A SHIPMAN and a PRIORESS!
      Sir Thopas (who he?)
      And this bloke Melibee,
And that should be enough, more or less!

That's forgetting that last but not least
Come MANCIPLE, MONK and NUN's PRIEST,
      PARSON and *SECOND* NUN,
      CANON's YEOMAN!! All done?
On the whole I'd avoid the southeast.

But to sum up each Canterbury Tale
Would require the lifespan of a whale
      (While hoping quite soon
      That you'd stop a harpoon).
I'd sooner start seeking the grail.

So just take it from me, on the whole,
Each nobleman, cleric or prole
      Gives CHAUCER his text
      By speaking of SEX!
(Called Courtly Love if you've a soul...)

But then, at the end of the road,
Geoff cops out with a PALINODE!
      ie. A retraction
      For all that hot action
Some of it with a commode.

As for Geoff's other work, it evokes
High Poetry rather than pokes.
      It's all much of a muchness,
      Though THE BOOK OF THE DUCHESS,
Like THE HOUSE OF FAME, leaves out the jokes....

Piers Plowman

There was a Fair Field Full of Folk
(Stick with it – this isn't a joke)
   Which was seen in a dream,
   A thing analysts deem
As psychotic. The dreamer awoke

And wrote down in trauma PIERS PLOWMAN,
A book most psychologists allow can
   Induce terrible fits
   As it bores you to bits
And the shrinks cry out 'Don't have a cow, man!'

Careful reading can maybe unbolt
That its subject's The Peasants' Revolt
   Though its thick Middle English
   Makes it hard to distinguish
If it's just about GOD. Oy gevalt!

Abandoning critical tools
For Freudian ones rightly appals,
   But any clinician
   Or diagnostician
Will conclude that PIERS PLOWMAN is balls!

Gawain and the Green Knight

There once was this chap called GAWAIN
Who beheads a Green Knight! What a pain.
        But the green git ain't dead
        And just picks up his head,
A party trick rivalling DAVE BLAINE!

A year on, GAWAIN's destiny
Is be paid back in kind! Dearie me.
        Though he's virtuous and brave,
        He seems set for the grave.
Who the *green* one is here we'll soon see.

But before the Green Knight's axe can hack
G. stays with *red* Sir BERTILAK.
        But then BERTILAK's missus
        Showers GAWAIN with kisses
Although they don't end in the sack.

In this kind of Romance the bed
Is eschewed. Will G's blood then run red
        Once beheaded? By 'eck,*
        Greenie just nicks his neck!
Which is what they meant by 'giving head'...

*If this usage looks weird on the page
The adaption's by S. ARMITAGE.

55

Scriptorium

To 14th C. Lit's jolly crew
We courteously bid our adieu.
        To CHAUCER, BOCCACCIOO
        And DANTE, attached to who
Are GOWER and WILL LANGLAND. Phew!

But recall that this opus, so grand,
Was all written out in longhand
        By scribes all unstinting
        Who didn't have printing.
This affected supply and demand.

True, limning a Capital letter a
Scribe could, in truth, not do betterer
        Stuck in his scriptorium
        But in an emporium
Like Waterstone's or Books Etc

The traders in books looked askance
At their stock – ONE THIN BOOK OF ROMANCE!
        And if that took a year
        To write down then it's clear
If you want 3 for 1 deals, fat chance!

The Fifteenth Century

We now make our rhythmical entry
Into LIT of the great 15th Century,
       When Geoffreys and Walters
       Penned Romance and Psalters
To serve up to Peasant and Gentry.

Except that... um...er... *To be frank*,
As to writers among the first rank
       And well worth their salary,
       Till we get to Malory
I'm afraid that my mind draws a blank.

For example, unless I'm quite wrong,
THE HUNDRED YEARS WAR, although long
       Spawned no bestselling star
       If you rule out FROISSART*,
Apart from the Agincourt Song.

So what's up? Were they suffering from fever
In this age of the underachiever?
       There's just no one who's GREAT,
       Except John Lydgate.
Who? THE SIEGE OF THEBES? Well? No, me neither.

*Doesn't count, as he wasn't alive
After 1405.

Le Morte D'Arthur

We've observed that after 1400
Lit flagged as society sundered
       With the Wars of the Roses.
       One only supposes
That writers then murdered and plundered.

Such a career is T. MALORY's
Who, rather than charming the galleries,
       Wrought havoc from Norwich
       To Kent and so porridge
Thereafter provided his calories.

Having got into many a scrape,
Like sheepstealing, murder and rape,
       Chucked in gaol, sans parole,
       He just rolled out a scroll
And wrote Chivalrous Tales as escape.

Is it justice, we ask, that this thug,
Having written MORTE D'ARTHUR in jug,
       Is rewarded with fame?
       With an ASBO the shame
Would have stopped the sod looking so smug.

Gutenberg

Great GUTENBERG (first name Johannes,
Who's to blame, in the long term, for scanners)
      Found that no kind of bribery
      Could convince his library
To lend him a book! Such bad manners

Were explained by the surly librarian
Who said, 'I'm not being contrarian.
      Books are rare and hand-made,
      And I know it sounds staid
But we're pre-industrial and agrarian!

Just think, in our World Medieval,
Of the terrible social upheaval
      Of MORE INFORMATION!
      Next stop – Reformation!
And our culture thus beyond retrieval!

So sling yer hook, mate, and don't gripe!
Mass-production? The time's not yet ripe!'
      Unmoved by this address
      Joe invented THE PRESS
To be difficult. You know the type.

Caxton

CAXTON cried to his girlfriend, 'Oh boy!
Here's some stuff for us both to enjoy!
       Just brace yerself, baby!
       Then afterwards, maybe,
I'll show you my HISTORYES OF TROYE!'

She replied, by the light of a taper,
'You can quite forget that kind of caper!'
       He rejoined, 'I won't force ya,
       But look at this CHAUCER,
And finger the weight of this paper!'

But the maiden remained unimpressed
And hissed 'Don't think I'm getting undressed
       And nor will I wipe
       From your moveable type
Any stuff that you get off your chest!'

And so there we leave poor WILL CAXTON
Who despite wishing that he'd relaxed on
       His Great Printing Press
       Was obliged to confess
That that wouldn't be what he climaxed on...

Printing

With GUTENBERG claiming paternity
The Printing Press ushered Modernity.
       Books had been rare and chained
       But now Lit, unrestrained
Could pass Mankind's thoughts to Eternity.

Just take Bibles. Though precious and numinous
With hand painted capitals luminous,
       After Printing + LUTHER
       Their Truth became TRUTHER
And, volume-wise, frankly voluminous.

Moreover, this paradigm leap
Made books widely spread and quite cheap
       So power passed to the PEOPLE
       From Castle and Steeple
Thanks to GUTENBERG. Christ, what a creep!

Because Printing is like a disease
(Just think of MEIN KAMPF, if you please)
       And monstrous plagues pale
       Besides the DAILY MAIL,
Irrespective of all those poor trees!

Bookselling

16th Century. A Bookseller squints
And says 'MACHIEVELLI's THE PRINCE
Is hot! Strewf! Those BORGIAS
            Were utterly gorgeous!'
Both of his customers wince.

'Sir. Madam. A very wise choice.
It's nasty, that book. But rejoice!
            'Ere's FOXE's BOOK OF MARTYRS,
            And that's just for starters!'
'No thank you,' his customers voice.

'All right then. I see you're both toffs.
CASTIGLIONE! No one scoffs
            At *his* work, so I've brought ya
            THE BOOK OF THE COURTIER!'
Each customer fidgets and coughs.

'Bloody 'ell, you're 'ard work!' 'We can pay.'
'Sir and Madam! Why didn't you say?
            I've got any amounta
            Stuff under the counter!'
'We'd like anything by RABELAIS...'*

*Critics may view my reasoning with scorn,
But the whole point of PRINTING is PORN!

Humanism

Post-printing and pre-Reformation
The presses of every nation
        Churned out poetry, tracts
        And histories; acts
Which led to new kinds of inflation.

Things inflated included the head
Of the author ERASMUS it's said,
        As this Humanist fellah
        Became a bestseller
And thus became truly well-read.

Though for struggling hacks on the make
In practice it proved a mistake
        To think FAME's the reward
        For we have to record
That TYNDALE was burned at the stake!

And likewise there's poor THOMAS MORE
Whose UTOPIA filled readers with awe.
        Then he hit writer's block
        And it came as no shock
When thereafter his head hit the floor.

World Lit

I must now confess to complicity
In fostering Eurocentricity!
        All the oeuvres in my rhymes
        Hail from Christendom's climes!
I'll correct this with abject felicity.

For ages World Lit has been found
To have powers to both awe and astound
        (Just take, for a starter
        THE MAHABHARATA)
Before most of us knew Earth was round.

Though eschewing conventional iamb
Lit from Araby, Cathay or Siam
        Or by Berbers or Persians
        Should be free of aspersions:
Think THE RUBAIYAT OF OMAR KHAYYAM!

And yet critics, when meeting in quorum
And asked for Lit's *victor ludorum*
        Name the Sweet Swan of Avon
        And, because they're craven,
As the rest are in foreign, ignore 'em.

Surrey! Wyatt?

1500s! Huzzah! And it's clear
That very soon we'll be quite near
       To SHAKESPEARE! The Bard!
       But although it's quite hard
There's some other blokes 'fore then, I fear.

Like JOHN SKELTON who lived in a garret
As poets must, and drank bad claret.
       Speke Budgerigar
       Didn't get him as far
As he got with his poem *Speke Parrot*.

THOMAS WYATT wrote sonnets all week
And gave Anne Boleyn's bottom a tweak!
       He got sent to The Tower!
       And within one brief hour
They fled him that once did him seek.

Worse awaited H. HOWARD, EARL of SURREY,
Who wrote sonnets too, in a hurry,
       Before *he* got beheaded!
       Though his poems weren't shredded,
So POSTERITY needn't worry...

Magi

In the Tudor Age, men were immersed
In new learning which magically burst
      On the world of the learned.
      These MAGI then earned
Dosh tutoring ELIZABETH the FIRST.

One such was the sage ROGER ASCHAM
Who, having great insights, would flash 'em
      At boys keen to learn,
      But if one boy did spurn
His methods he'd naturally thrash 'em.

Likewise, there's the Magus JOHN DEE
Who would summon angels round for tea
      Through dabbling alchemical
      Though these beings chimerical
Were quite safe – it was necroMANCY...

But the Queen cried 'Dee! I need a mate or
The Tudors are toast! Our Creator
      Needs HEIRS, so don't plague us
      With more Magi, Magus!'
(Though the magazine MY GUY came later...)

UM, WHAT KIND OF MAGICIAN DID YOU SAY YOU WERE AGAIN, DR DEE?

Astrophel and Stella

There once was a courtier called SIDNEY
(SIR PHILIP, in fact, of that kidney).
            ASTROPHEL AND STELLA
            Was his best-known bestseller.
But one wonders, well, did he or didne?

Get his rocks off with STELLA, that is.
I suppose that that's none of our biz.
            For these sonnets and songs
            Are too courtly. One longs
For some ruff bump and grind! What a swizz!

Romantically, SIDNEY's prestige
Hit the roof when, shot down in a siege,
            He died (he's been poorly);
            His friend WALTER RALEGH*
Asked the Queen, 'A Potato, my liege?'

SIR WALT also brought to Queen Bess
TOBACCO to ease her distress.
            But though fags now dismay us,
            She cried '20 PLAYERS
And SHAG!' Walt just dropped his cloak! Bless!

*The pronunciation changes hourly,
So it's *Ralegh* or *Ralegh* or *Ralegh*.

The Faerie Queen

There once was a poet called SPENSER
So smart that he could've joined MENSA!
       He wrote EPITHALAMION
       (How sesquepaedalian)
And invented the soft drink dispenser.

That last bit's a lie, though it rhymes.
But honestly, how many times
       Can the Sweete Thames run softly
       In cadences loftly?
And that's not the least of his crimes.

In THE FAERIE QUEEN he would refine
The flattering arts to define
       Queen Bess – 'Gloriana' –
       As top top banana
In line after *line* after *LINE*!

There's paynims, a Bowre of Bliss,
Knights and dwarves – was he taking the piss?
       But although, to his credit,
       No one's ever read it,
On the whole I'd give this one a miss.

The Spanish Tragedy

There once was this kid name of KYD
Who wrote stuff for the early to mid
        Elizabethan theatre
        Which frankly appeared ter
Come screaming straight out of his id

In the way that he lifted the lid
On dark doings quite close to Madrid
        In his SPANISH TRAGEDY
        With chaps clannish badgered (the
REVENGE the pro quo for the quid).

So there's murder and madness amid
So much blood that you're likely to skid,
        Plus a bloke whose son's hung
        So he bites out his tongue
Which flops round on the stage like a squid.

Prudes think that drama should be rid
Of such things which are better left hid.
        But before TARANTINO
        You won't see a beano
Like this, so get down with the Kyd!

Marprelate

Just after the Spanish Armada
The extremes of Liturgical ardour
      Sparked a WAR OF THE PAMPHLETS
      Where each rival camp gets
More flouncy than students at RADA.

The way that the PURITANS tell it
The Bishops were heading for Hell! It
      Was all down to sin
      Which they pointed out in
THE LETTERS OF MARTIN MARPRELATE.

In response poets LYLY and NASHE
Were paid by the bishops to bash
      The agents of schism!
      They used EUPHUISM,
Which brought poor NASHE out in a rash!

In agony NASHE cried, 'Oh LYLY!
Just look at the state of my willy!
      I'm hard-line C of E.
      But right now I can't pee!'
LYLY said, '*Nonny no, dilly dilly.*'

Marlowe

There once was this a playwright called KIT
Who packed 'em in using his wit
> Plus some violence and iamb
> So the tickets, they'd buy 'em
Meaning hit after hit after hit!

So there's *FAUSTUS* with HELEN of TROY
And *TAMBURLAINE* and, though a goy,
> Young KIT didn't falter
> At *THE JEW OF MALTA*!
I mean, what's there not to enjoy?

Then there's *EDWARD II*! A side, though,
Of Marlowe emerges here: slide, oh,
> That poker, red hot,
> Into poor Eddy's bot!
(Though one reading insists it's a *DIDO*.)

But then this gay atheist spy
And tragedian, mid hue and cry
> Got murdered in DEPTFORD!
> Is FATE so inept? Would
You choose this dump where to die?

The Elizabethan Theatre

With ELIZABETH entering her senescence
Playwrights forged a dramatical RENAISSANCE.
       Have you thought (and you should)
       Why anyone would
Have given these wasters a second glance?

For once they had had to resort
To writing dull masques for the court,
       But then ALLEYN and BURBAGE
       Released all this verbiage
To the public at large! Who'd've thought?

They built theatres – Great Wooden Os –
And stumped up the cash for the shows
       (ALLEYN owned a brothel)
       So paid for this waffle
To be played in a doublet and hose.

Thanks to BURBAGE and ALLEYN above we
See GENIUS and TRADE hand in glove free
       Great Art from neglect!
       (Which is what you'd expect
From each frightful old prototype luvvy...)

Dekker

The playwright and hack THOMAS DEKKER
(Who was ignorant of the spell-checker)
       Was churning out plays
       When his indolent gaze
Espied a bulge caused by his pecker.

'Forsooth!' he exclaimed, 'I've a MARSTON!
On reflection, I'd better have passed on
       That meddlesome chore
       Writing THE HONEST WHORE!
The groundlings will be left aghast! On

The other hand, I too can gauge
The theatrical tone of the age:
       So should I appear
       On stage shaking my spear
God only knows who I'd upstage!'

Nonetheless DEKKER chose to disrobe
As the candlelight started to strobe
       And exposed his BEN JONSON
       And thus was his swansong
At the end of Act V at The Globe!

Shakespeare's Contemporaries

I don't doubt that ASHTON and ARMIN
And ALABASTER were quite charmin'
       And BRANDON and BROME
       Could delight a whole room
While GLAPHORNE was frankly disarmin',

And HOUGHTON and LIPTON and HUGHES
Wrote stuff that packed plebs in the pews
       While PRESTON and PEELE
       Made the audience squeal
And FIELD never fumbled his cues,

And CARLELL and CARTWRIGHT and CHETTLE
Penned plays that were bound to unsettle
       The groundlings in shows
       At The Globe and The Rose!
Each playwright, in excellent fettle,

Delivered the goods, and quite fast,
Though they're all NOW FORGOTTEN. This cast,
       When compared to SHAKESPEARE
       Make it horribly clear
That none of them should've been arsed....

Shakespeare's World

Consider a baker who bakes. Here
Is some fool who tempts you with cakes. Jeer
      At this fatuous food.
      It won't alter your mood,
So just hope beyond hope there's a jakes near.

Likewise with all drink your thirst slakes – beer,
Bacardi or gin – for God's sake, steer
      Away from all booze!
      It won't chase off the blues
But instead bring headaches and the shakes, dear.

Instead think of ART, for this makes clear
How to SUCCOUR THE SOUL! (Watch for fakes; fear
      The low poetaster:
      He'll lead to disaster!
Far better to drown in a lake's weir!)

But though philistines, dullards and rakes sneer
At POETRY, ignore these snakes! Hear
      THE CALL OF THE MUSE
      And then rip off yer trews
AND LET'S GET STUCK IN TO SOME SHAKESPEARE!

THE COMPLETE WORKS OF SHAKESPEARE

The Taming of the Shrew

An old man of Padua's daughters
Would be wed, but as protocol's taught us,
      KATE (the elder) weds first
      So BIANCA is cursed
To bide her time in spinster's quarters.

It's a play, so there's clearly a spoiler.
From big sis all suitors recoil! The
      Truth is that KATE
      Is devoured by hate
For men! She's a right bunny boiler!

B.'s boyfriend sees hope of a porkin'
Receding, and so he starts talkin'
      PETRUCHIO, his mate
      Into having a date
With Kate, aka ANDREA DWORKIN.

KATE gets tamed, which she learns to accept. Good
And docile is now her precept. Could
      Any fellow resist her?
      She's just like her sister
In Padua! (Sounds more like Stepford...)

Two Gentlemen of Verona

There once were two gents of Verona
And one of these gents got a boner
        For sweet constant JULIA
        So it's hardly peculiar
His chum left for Milan, a loner,

Where he fell for fair SILVIA. What joy!
Though GENT ONE then arrived and – oy oy! –
        Was immediately smitten
        By this stunning sex kitten
And then JULES arrived – dressed as a boy!

Then SILV's captured by brigands! It's curious
That FIRST GENT now rescues her. Spurious
        Sexual harassment
        Leads to embarrassment,
Leaving Jules and GENT TWO frankly furious!

But though each of 'em's clearly a goer
It sorts itself out. End of show. A
        Play much less confusing
        But just as amusing
Might've been *The ONE Gent of Genoa...*

King Henry VI parts 1, 2 and 3

HENRY VI, in Parts I, II and III,
Were penned, ahistorically,
       About six years before
       Parts of KING HENRY IV
And eight years before HENRY V.*

GLOUCESTER, WARWICK and YORK, with elation
Fight SUFFOLK and BEDFORD. The nation
       Is soon strewn with dead
       (It's all in HOLINSHED)
Though it sounds more like sat-navigation.

Meanwhile MARGARET OF ANJOU runs rings
Around TALBOT and MORTIMER. Things
       Just go round and round
       HENRY sits on the ground
And tells stories about fallen kings.

In these early plays future fame beckoned
To SHAKESPEARE, though most critics reckoned
       Arithmetically
       Six divided by three
Meant it should have been *HENRY THE SECOND*.

*This makes sense in iambic pentameter
To scholars, but not to the amateur...

Richard III

The HISTORY OF RICHARD THE THIRD
Is tragic but slightly absurd.
       SHAKESPEARE's too rude as
       He bigs up the Tudors
And writes stuff that never occurred.

The play starts with a weather forecast.
Winter's gone. Now there's sunshine at last!
       But though YORK's sun is shining
       DUKE RICHARD's repining.
He isn't king yet! Damn and blast!

Soon the Malmsey butts' surfaces ripple
And young princes are croaked by this cripple.
       (If not being PC
       Isn't your cup of tea
Recall blood was the cruel hunchback's tipple.)

Then the tables are turned, and it's fabled
Dick called for a horse, loose or stabled,
       For although a bad sort
       In equestrian sport
He's a role model for the disabled!

The Comedy of Errors

There once was this family from Syracuse
And did ever choirmaster choir abuse
        Twin boys with such shame?
        They both had the same name!
But before the shocked audience cry '*j'accuse*!'

We get even nearer the knuckle
As we watch how the poor lads' bad luck'll
        Find them tossed on the waves
        With *identical slaves!*
Only stone-hearted cynics would chuckle.

There's a ship wreck. Does Davy Jones' locker
Welcome boy, slave and mum? What a shocker!
        The survivors (you've guessed)
        Disappear on a quest
To find them. Dad goes off his rocker.

As each fresh disaster divides
These poor people, what title provides
        A fit name for these terrors?
        THE COMEDY OF ERRORS!
Oh right. Ha ha ha. Split my sides.

Titus Andonicus

We now come to TITUS ANDRONICUS,
The violence in which is a tonic as
        It shows people with faults
        And is quite free from schmaltz
Just like life! (Or at least ERICH HONECKER's.)

In short, Titus makes sacrifice
Of TAMORA the Goth's son. Not nice.
        So with AARON THE MOOR
        And a lakeful of gore
The play shows us the whole of life's spice!

Tam's sons rape LAVINIA and
Cut her tongue out and chop off each hand.
        L's dad Tite (this is peach)
        Bakes both boys in a quiche
Which TAMORA eats! Isn't life grand?

TAMORA cries, 'Yuk! Bloody Nora!
I'll puke!' But T. says, 'I implore ya!
        Don't be sick! Play it canny
        Or we'll look just like *ANNIE*
And *both sons'll come out, Tamora!*'

Romeo and Juliet

TWO HOUSEHOLDS, alike dignified,
Would oft in Verona collide
      And the CAPULET crew
      Would cry 'Screw MONTAGUE!'
'Screw *you!*' the MONTAGUES replied.

Then ROMEO, a Montague, crashes
One of the CAPULETS' bashes,
      Falls for JULES (aged 13),
      Runs her kinsman through clean
And thereafter out of town dashes.

FRIAR LAWRENCE says 'Juliet Capulet,
Do you want to get off with that chap you met?
      Will you come to the crypt
      Feigning death, so the script
Means the fan won't get hit by the crap?' 'You bet!'

When he should've stayed home at his mother's,
Thinking J.'s dead, R drinks poison! Others
      Find Juliet!
      Stabbed herself! (Was upset.)
Life's a bitch for these two star-cross'd lovers...

Love's Labours Lost

There once was a KING of NAVARRE
Who exiled chicks from his boudoir
       With three of his lords
       Who foreswore all broads
For study and fasting! Bizarre.

Then the PRINCESS OF FRANCE – ooh la la! –
And three of her babes reach Navarre.
       The king and his chummies
       Then fall for these yummies
And yearn to take off each girl's bra.

Ere they can take petting too far
We gets subplots and scholars who are
       Seen endlessly chattin'
       In very bad Latin
Plus COSTARD THE CLOWN. Ha ha ha!

Delayed by a play in the play
Before anyone gets it away
       The KING OF FRANCE dies!
       'Wait a year!' PRINCESS cries.
Do you think they might all have been gay?

Richard II

We now come to RICHARD THE SECOND
Whose grandad, ED THREE, was so fecund
      His son, JOHN OF GAUNT
      Was Dick's uncle (not aunt).
In this family Tragedy beckoned

When BOLINBROKE (Gaunt's son, Dick's cousin)
Quarrels, fifteen to the dozen
      With MOWBRAY (a duke)
      And thus earns the rebuke
Of exile from Dick. Things are buzzin'!

Gaunt speaks about this sceptred isle,
This England, this blessed plot while
      He's dying! The strength
      To go on at such length
Is amazing in someone senile.

When Dick steals Gaunt's land Bol, Gaunt's son
Returns home and Dick's soon on the run
      And because he's unequal
      To Kingship the sequel
Isn't *DICK III* but *HENRY IV (I)*...

A Midsummer Night's Dream

In Athenian woods take a gander
At HELENA, HERMIA, LYSANDER
    And DEMETRIUS, vowed
    To Herm, who is wowed
By Lys (Hel wants Dem). A bystander

Might then observe, while being wary,
TITANIA and OBERON vary
    Over the fate
    Of a changeling. 'Look mate,'
Says Tit. 'Do your worst, you big fairy!'

So Ob summons PUCK so he'll twit
TITANIA with *pansies!* The git
    Spoils BOTTOM's am-dram
    With an ASS's HEAD scam
And soon things go Ass over TIT.

All's sorted out. Our lovers deem
The mechanicals' play a right scream,
    Though I think it's callous
    To pinch tricks from *DALLAS*
And say the whole thing was a dream...

King John

SHAKESPEARE, the soul of his age,
Cast genius o'er page after page
      Nor e'er blotted a line
      Which is perfectly fine
But in order to rattle his cage

We should point out that some of his plays
Signally fail to amaze.
      If you've seen, say, *KING JOHN*
      Then you'll think 'What a con!'
With regret to the end of your days.

KING JOHN, play and man, were both bad
But Tudor types thought that this cad
      Was OK cos the dope
      Had a tiff with the Pope
And was therefore a right jack the lad.

Maybe SHAKESPEARE was stuck in a rut
When he wrote it. In his final cut
      There's no Magna Carta!
      Is this serving true art or
The work of a brown-nosing slut?

The Merchant of Venice

Though BASSANIO loves PORTIA, he's broke
So can't court her. The chance of a poke
  Needs a loan from mate TONY
  But Tony is stoney!
SHYLOCK in his gabardine cloak

Says if Tone stands a bond, then a loan
Is forthcoming, though SHYLOCK hates Tone!
  'By my gabardine raiments,
  The only repayment's
A *POUND OF FLESH*, all of your own!'

Bass weds. Tone defaults. S. complained
And called in his debt! Thus arraigned
  Stand the JEW and the GOY as
  They wheel in the lawyers!
Will the quality of mercy be strained?

PORTIA, dressed as a lawyer this time,
Says, '*You spilla da blood, issa crime!*'
  Shylock's foiled by the tricksa
  This cross-dressing shiksa.
He should have tried lending sub-prime...

Henry IV part 1

In HENRY THE FOURTH (the first part)
Things are going downhill from the start!
       HENRY's son, young PRINCE HAL
       Larks and whores with his pal
JOHN FALSTAFF, a drunken old fart.

He should have been glad for small mercies,
For HENRY's now harried by PERCIES
       And the chutzpah of HOTSPUR!
       How can HENRY prosper?
When things couldn't get any worse he's

Surrounded by foes by the hour –
There's MORTIMER, WORCESTER, GLENDOWER
       And DOUGLAS THE SCOT!
       But Hal quits as a sot
And swaps sack for the prospect of power!

Who's fighting who? Haven't a clue.
Then Hal runs his mate HOTSPUR through
       At the Battle of Shrewsbury
       Where FALSTAFF plays gooseberry.
For the climax please wait for Part II...

Henry IV part 2

In HENRY THE FOURTH's second part
The various goings-on chart
       How PRINCE HAL becomes king
       But enjoys a last fling.
Dad thinks Hal's bound for Hell in a cart.

For the King, lying on his deathbed,
Sees Hal plonk the crown on his own head.
       'Feckless lout!' the King cries
       But then, reconciled, dies.
Once more this is all in HOLINSHED.

Meanwhile FALSTAFF is now overjoyed
(Though his exploits would shame a tabloid)
       That Hal's King! 'I'm in clover!'
       But ere the play's over
He's spurned. This stuff's straight out of FREUD!

Thus FALSTAFF's fate humbly proposes
That boozers, with bad halitosis,
       Can piss up with princes
       But *not* Kings. One winces.
The next stop's THE WARS OF CIRRHOSIS...

Much Ado About Nothing

In the play MUCH ADO ABOUT NOTHING
There's a great deal of huffing and puffing
   Whether true love is pure
   So we have to endure
Five Acts with no signs of a stuffing!

Here's CLAUDIO who's obviously gagging
But from the start chances of shagging
   The beautiful HERO
   Appear to be zero
Cos DON PEDRO woos her. (He's ragging.)

That's resolved, but before we're half through
DON JOHN's scheming sets things askew
   And true love seems to falter!
   H is spurned at the altar
So feigns death, as heroines do.

But before you can hope to unpick
The plot DOGBERRY does his shtik.
   Hero comes back to life.
   CLAUDIO makes her his wife.
And BEATRICE gets some (Bene)dick!

Henry V

SHAKESPEARE acknowledges a wooden O
Quite clearly and obviously cooden show
   VASTY FIELDS OF FRANCE
   So if given a chance
Any sensible audience shooden go.

But in HENRY THE FIFTH there's a CHORUS
Who with his muse of fire doth implore us
   To piece out imperfection
   With thought's recollection
Of horses on grass and such floras.

So it's off to France! Straight off the beach
We're once more, chums, unto the breach!
   So please cry God for Harry
   (Either KENNETH or LARRY)
Bashing frogs with another great speech!

Then there's PISTOL and all of that crew
And news FALSTAFF's dead. Boo hoo hoo!
   Plus a glorious glut
   Of Frenchified smut!
As Harry says: 'We happy... *phew!*'

Julius Caesar

In Rome JULIUS CAESAR's ambition
Leads CASSIUS, lean hungry patrician,
  To cajole MARCUS BRUTUS
  To brutally refute as
A fact CAESAR's breathing condition.

But BRUTUS is HONOURABLE. Deciding
Is hard. Then a soothsayer's chiding
  Jules C. neath an arch.
  'Beware the Ides of March!
'Cos you're cruising, mate, for a good 'iding!'

BRUTUS strikes, HONOURABLY, for the nation
And CAESAR dies with a quotation.
  'Et tu, Brute?' His timing
  (Somewhere close a clock's chiming)
Is surpassed by MARK TONY's oration.

'Friends Romans and Countrymen! CAESAR's
Been topped! Here's the best of us geezers
  Croaked by HONOURABLE men!'
  Who are soon dead too. Then
Tone says *BRUTUS* was NOBLEST! Jesus!

As You Like It

Duke Fred, in the play AS YOU LIKE IT,
Having told the real duke, 'on yer bike!', it
        Transpires, lets Duke's daughter
        (Blood's thicker than water)
Stay at court, though she soon takes a hike. It

Gets worse. ROS (of whom we just spoke)
Like most heroines fancies a poke
        From ORLANDO, her lover,
        Who's fled from his brother
And Ros is now dressed as a bloke.

Soon they're all in the FOREST OF ARDEN:
Ros as GANYMEDE (I beg your pardon?),
        Courtiers, fools, shepherdesses
        And each one confesses
TRUE LOVE – even Ros has a harden!

In the end, as a drunk coulda tol' ya,
All's resolved, although JACQUES' melancholia*
        Makes this misery engage
        All the World as a stage,
Or so it says in the First Folia...

*This scansion depends if one takes
The pronouncing of 'Jacques' as 'Jacques'...

Hamlet

Prince HAMLET the Dane's murdered dad,
Haunting battlements says, 'Listen, lad,
   I was croaked by my brother
   Who's married your mother!
Avenge me!' So feigning he's mad

Young HAMLET now seeks to embarrass
His mum, and to sexually harass
   OPHELIA! 'Just run,'
   He sneers. 'Go be a nun!'
And then stabs her poor pa through the arras!

She goes mad and soon Death doth collect her.
With a fool's skull (a funeral director
   Was sloppy) this student
   Decides it's imprudent
To kill himself. HANNIBAL LECTER

Would blanche once the whole cast's deployed
Poisoned blades! And now woe's unalloyed:
   Step-dad's stabbed; HAMLET's hurt; he's
   Soon dead; so's LAERTES.
And good morning to *you*, DR FREUD!

Twelfth Night

By 12th night the weather gets chillier,
And shipwrecked in coastal ILLYRIA
       VIOLA, in drag
       Must help ORSINO bag
OLIVIA. Then it gets sillier.

For starters VIOLA's a twin.
Then OLIVIA falls for her in
       The belief she's a chap.
       V. Loves ORSINO! Crap!
While MALVOLIO's trying to win

Liv's love! BELCH has made him suppose
If her wears yellow cross gartered hose
       He'll succeed. Fate's tombola
       Marks him as bi-polar!
V.'s twin brother SEB turns up! Woes

Turn suddenly to celebrations!
(Illyria's now home to CROATIANS.
       On 12th night, if you please,
       They just chuck out their trees
And ignore the play's gay connotations...)

The Merry Wives of Windsor

SIR JOHN FALSTAFF, broke, doth avow
His love for two wealthy hausfrau
      In a play that's a prequel
      To a previous sequel
And the whole thing takes place quite near Slough.

Eyeing up Mistresses PAGE and FORD
The fat nincompoop thinks he's scored,
      Although these merry wives
      Are both brought out in hives
When they think of SIR JOHN. His reward

Is to be bundled up in the wash
And then chucked in the Thames with a splosh!
      (Oh! I nearly forgot!
      There's a complex sub-plot
About ANNE PAGE, but that's also tosh.)

Then this ancestor of BILLY BUNTER
Gets dressed up as... HERNE THE HUNTER
      In Windsor Great Park!
      Gets duffed up! What a lark!
My very sides splitteth asunder.

Troilus and Cressida

We know Shakespeare's TROILUS AND CRESSIDA
Is a 'problem play'. No one can guessida
       What this tale, set in Troy
       (It's just girl lost by boy)
Is about. Nonetheless, I confessida

The problem's much deeper. The source
Of this play of betrayal and remorse
       Ain't Greek but Medieval
       Though Troy's great upheaval
Does not even *mention* the HORSE!

It's gets far, far worse, I'm afraid.
Does TROILUS actually get laid
       By CRESSIDA? The source (a
       Long poem by CHAUCER)
Insists the dame's real name's CRISEYDE!

This confusion of historicism
Occludes our sight through a dark prism
       Although maybe it's true
       It's not one chick, but two,
And he should've been called TROILISM...

All's Well That Ends Well

In Shakespeare's play ALL'S WELL THAT ENDS WELL,
HELENA, whose family and friends smell
       As the girl's of low birth
       Will move Heaven and Earth
To win BERT! Will it work? That depends. Hell!

The snob looks on HELEN askance!
Love seems doomed, but she grabs the main chance
       Using medical skills
       To cure fistula ills
Of Bert's guardian, who's KING OF FRANCE.

In payment she gets to wed Bert
Who sods off to war with a curt
       Note saying maybe
       If he fathers her baby
And she fingers his ring he might flirt.

But, as they say, all's well that ends well
For HELENA, in bed, pretends, well,
       She's DIANA, Bert's doxy
       And therefore, by proxy,
She finally makes BERTRAM's end swell.

Measure for Measure

CLAUDIO, in MEASURE FOR MEASURE,
Breaks the sex laws in moments of leisure
        With JULIET enough
        To get her up the duff,
So's condemned to death at the Duke's pleasure.

C.'s judge is ANGELO, a liar.
(The DUKE's off disguised as a friar.)
        C.'s sis, the nun BELLA
        Intercedes for the fellah
But it's frying pan into the fire.

You see, MERCY will cost her her cherry,
And for a nun this measure's very
        Inconvenient (and sick)
        So she pulls a 'bed trick'!
MARIANNA makes Angelo merry!

But ANGELO still wants C. dead,
And demands his bonce! It has been said
        This is Will's 'problem play'
        But it ends up okay
With a nun and a judge 'giving head'!

Othello

OTHELLO's a Moor whose amour
For DESDEMONA ends in gore
       Thanks to wicked IAGO.
       This entire farrago
Piles up corpses ten foot from the floor.

For it happens that sweet DESDEMONA
Has also occasioned a boner
       In a certain RODRIGO
       While Iago's ego
Is affronted by CASSIO! Phone a

Friend! Ask the audience! How
Can IAGO conspire to allow
       Everything to turn manky
       Because Des's HANKY
Gets nicked by Ig's wife, the daft cow?

Is this play about RACE, or the blows
That we reap, and which JEALOUSY sows?
       Or is the real issue
       You should use a tissue –
Not a handkerchief – blowing your nose?

King Lear

LEAR demands his three daughters declare
Their love so his realm they can share.
   Only two come up trumps
   (GON and REGAN – both frumps)
But CORDELIA's cut off! Is this fair?

Meanwhile EDMUND (a bastard) can't see
Why EDGAR's legitimacy
   Makes his big bro seem better
   So he forges a letter
And their dad thus dumps EDGAR! Dear me!

Then GON and REG, both social climbers,
Kick out Lear who sinks into Alzheimer's
   On the heath. EDGAR's feigning
   He's mad – *and it's raining!*
Lear's FOOL observes, 'For us old timers

We're better off staying indoors!
But now everyone's dead Fate implores
   That the skies are enraged!
   Please, let's call Help the Aged!
Nuncle, you never reign but it pours!'

Macbeth

The Scottish usurper MACBETH
With his antepenultimate breath
        Cried out 'Lay on, MACDUFF!
        Frankly I've had enough
Of all of this witchcraft and death!

'When a Focus Group (each one a hag)
Said I had Scotland's crown in the bag
        My dear wife's ambition
        Said this high position
Meant murdering the king! What a drag!

'They said BANQUO would sire lines of kings,
So I murdered him too. Several things
        Resulted: his ghost
        Ruined my beans on toast
And my wife started sleepwalking! Jings!

'They said, "Of forest armies beware
Plus men not born of women!" Oh yeah?
        But Caesarian section?!
        I'm stuffed!' On reflection,
Is this how focus groups did for BLAIR?

Antony and Cleopatra

MARK ANTONY said with a smile
'I don't care if I'm boss in Rome! I'll
       Stay with CLEOPATRA
       Transported in rapture!
Sod OCTAVIUS! I'm in de Nile!'

'Just look at her barge and her garb as
It reminds me somehow of rhubarb as
       That's long, pink and parts
       Of it go into tarts!'
Says Tony's great mate ENOBARBUS.

Then Tone marries OCTAVIUS's sister!
Cleo's cross! Tone returns (can't resist 'er).
       This means war! But the flight
       Of C's fleet mean the shite
Hits the ostrich plumed fan of this twister.

Tony falls on his sword, but askance,*
And then dies in C.'s arms. What Romance!
       Leaving Cleo to clasp
       To her bosom an ASP
Though preferring the snake in Tone's pants.

*For this verse to work everyone needs
To adopt the locution of Leeds...

Coriolanus

Politics can both free and enchain us
And sometimes even entertain us
> When Patricians and Plebs
> Get seduced by Celebs!
In a nutshell that's CORIOLANUS!

CORIOLANUS had biffed the Volscean
And earned himself many a paean
> Of praise, so his mum*
> Said 'Get to the For-um
And get elected!' He's not ke-en

But filled with pride says, 'I'm the flashest!
Vote for me, stinking plebs!' That's the rashest
> Slogan they've heard.
> The Plebs give him the bird,
Concluding the man is a fascist!

He swaps sides. Attacks Rome. But mayhem
Is averted when his mum (hem-hem)*
> Says, 'Son, please re-rat!
> Does. Gets killed. And that's that.
Do you think he'd have voted Lib Dem?

*He loved his mum, but there's no sex,
Just violence. More *Oedipus Wrecks.*

114

Timon of Athens

Have you heard about TIMON the Greek
Who banqueted all through the week,
      Spending every last penny
      On every and any
False friend who turned up? What a geek!

But then when his own credit rating
Went down the pan no friends were waiting.
      Cursing every knave
      He now lived in a cave
Where he found gold! (But carried on hating...)

Flush once more it now seems it's required he's
Loose with his cash! ALCIBIADES
      Takes a slice to attack
      The Athenians! Alack!
TIMON's dead 'neath the stars! (They're the *pleiades*.)

But everyone hates social climbin'!
Were things that much harder for TIMON?
      After all, lucky chap
      Wasn't told he was crap
On the X Factor by COWELL, SIMON...

Pericles, Prince of Tyre

PERICLES, young Prince of Tyre,
Gently began to perspire
       'Cos ANTICHUS's riddle
       Revealed he did fiddle
With his own *daughter*! Leave it out, squire!

King Ant sends assassins to slot
Our Perry, who scarpers. Who'd not?
       He saves TARSUS from famine
       And next weds a gamine
He wins in a joust! Then the plot

Gets confusing. His wife dies at sea
Giving birth – in a storm. Obviously.
       She gets chucked overboard
       But she's still alive! Gawd!
Then becomes a priestess! That's Act III.

Their daughter, meanwhile, has alighted
In Tarsus; skips death; ain't delighted
       When she's sold to a brothel!
       Two more acts of this waffle
Suggest SHAKESPEARE did not even write it!*

* Scholars differ on if it's canonical.
No wonder. It reads like McGonagall.

Cymbeline

CYMBELINE, an Ancient Briton,
Thought his daughter's marriage was unfittin'
     So he exiles the oik
     Who then concludes, 'Loike,
Moy woife's with some other bloke smitten!'

Soon everyone's badly behavin'
And in a cave in MILFORD HAVEN
     The crossdressing wife
     DIES and COMES BACK TO LIFE!
Could Shakespeare be really so craven?

'Golden lads and lasses all must,
As chimney sweepers, come to dust'
     Are the play's two good lines
     And this duly consigns
The rest to remain undiscussed.

Save that we all know *WINDOW-LENE*
Leaves your windows all sparkly and clean.
     If this tiresome frolic
     Is actually symbolic
Then it needs some more *SYMBOL-LENE!*

The Winter's Tale

LEONTES, the King of Sicilia
Towards his wife grows ever chillier
       Imaging she's
       Poking POLIXENES
And the plot gets increasingly sillier.

HERMIONE the wife's chucked in clink
Where she gives birth, then dies! Do you think
       When her kid's left to die
       On *Bohemia's coast* by
This point SHAKESPEARE's taken to drink?

For Bohemia's landlocked! No map
Shows a coastline for oceans to lap!
       Then sixteen years later
       The kid's long dead mater
Is a *statue!!* This whole thing is crap!

When the statue *comes back to life* where
Do we think the plot's gone? Do we care?
       If the audience is wise
       It'll just shut its eyes
And exit, pursued by a bear...

King Henry VIII

SHAKESPEARE, on The Globe's empty stage,
Forlornly perused a blank page
        And thought 'Some remission
        From this damned commission
Is what I deserve at my age!

'This latest gig – KING HENRY EIGHT –
Is hackwork! Is this now my fate,
        Simply to hand a
        Piece of propaganda
To the Court of KING JAMES on a plate?

'When Posterity weighs up my name
Far better plays should win me fame!
        Like *HAMLET*! Please fetch a
        Co-author! JOHN FLETCHER
Will do, and then he'll take the blame!'

(ENVOI: On the play's opening night
A prop set the theatre alight.
        This playhouse, in the round,
        Promptly burnt to the ground!
For a critic, a heartening sight!)

The Tempest

PROSPERO, ex-duke of Milan*
Spent years on an island just chillin'
      Till a TEMPEST he sends,
      For the answer, my friends,
Is blown in the wind (*qua* BOB DYLAN).

The storm (wrought by magic) then whisks
Prosp's usurping brother's ship! Risks
      Befall shipwrecked boyses;
      The isle's full of noises
But *not* like Des-ert Island Discs.

Prosp's 'guiled nephew FERDINAND's eyes
Behold cousin MIRANDA. Things rise,
      Though Prosp's tame spirit ARIEL
      Shows what a fairy'll
Say: *'Dad full fathom five lies!'*

All ends happily, though the plot's boggy
And several sailors get groggy
      As does monstrous CALIBAN
      Who's pissed (he's no Taliban)
And PROSPERO's library gets soggy.

* This pronunciation's been played on
But we are such stuff dreams are made on...

The Two Noble Kinsmen

When SHAKESPEARE at last took his bow
Did he leave the stage to a loud 'WOW!'?
        Did the cheers and the laughter
        Collide with each rafter
Of the house for his last play? Well, now...

He could've just capped his career
With *HAMLET 2* or *YOUNG KING LEAR*
        Or similar works
        Like *REVENGE OF THE TURKS*
(A sequel to *OTHELLO*); it's clear

That *MACBETH VERSUS CORIOLANUS*
Would've done, and it only can pain us
        That *JULIET: SEX KITTEN*
        Remains yet unwritten;
Is *TEMPTATION TEMPEST* that heinous?

But *THE TWO NOBLE KINSMEN?* Dear me!
Yet through a glass darkly I see
        WILL say to young FLETCHER,
        'You'll write it?' 'You betcha!'
Then WILL says: 'We'll still split the fee...'

The Sonnets

All the World's a Stage! And sat upon it
Is SHAKESPEARE! So please toss your bonnet
        Or cap in the air!
        He wrote drama with flair
Plus the occasional sonnet.

To a summer's day shall I compare thee?
That sums it all up pretty fairly.
        See how Shakespeare confines
        Within just 14 lines
All human thought that's airy-fairy.

Like most poems they're all about Truth
And Beauty and Love. And Death. Strewf!
        And while some were penned
        To a dark lady friend
Most were wrote to a beautiful youth.

He wrote with a quill, not a PC
(He was *Shakespeare*, you fool! Not KEN KESEY)
        And I'm not being rude
        If I'm forced to conclude
That Shakespeare was... well... AC/DC...

The Phoenix and the Turtle

As TIME ever onward doth hurtle
Through meadows of clover and myrtle
       We now wave goodbye
        To SHAKESPEARE. But fie!
I forgot *The Phoenix and the Turtle!*

There once was a turtle and phoenix
Which sounds to me like an obscene mix,
       Though the turtle's a *dove!*
        It must be about LOVE!
Best then to get out the kleenix.

Its meaning's obscure: do these fowl
As they die with a fiery howl
       Denote LOVE, TRUTH or BRAVERY
        Or RUNNING AN AVIARY
Or laying it on with a trowel?

Who cares? To be frank I'm too busy. Call
Time on old Will. Don't be quizzical,
       For *poetry*, you'll find,
        Pales beside *bump 'n' grind*
So, baby, let's get METAPHYSICAL!

To be continued...